Singing in the Stone Age

We do not know what songs people sang in the Stone Age. They might not have had songs at all. Instead, people might have used their voices to copy the calls that animals made. Some present-day hunters call animals towards them, such as birds, by imitating the sounds they make.

Cave music

Remains of musical instruments have been found in caves. These include drums made from shoulder-blades, rattles made from jawbones and xylophones made from hip bones. One instrument was called a bull-roarer. It was a flat piece of bone that was swung on a cord to make a loud roaring noise.

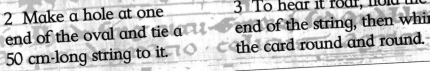

Make a bull-roarer

1 Draw an oval on thick card, about 20 cm x 10 cm, and cut it out.

2 Make a hole at one end of the oval and tie a 50 cm-long string to it.

3 To hear it roar, hold the end of the string, then whirl the card round and round.

In ancient times

Around 5,000 years ago, singing and dancing were part of daily life in Ancient Egypt and Mesopotamia (roughly where present-day Iraq is). There are pictures still in existence today that show how people danced, and musical instruments have also been found.

Egyptian musicians and dancers perform at a banquet. The musicians are clapping, and one blows a wind instrument.

Dance like an Egyptian

Ancient Egyptian dances were very acrobatic and full of energy. Dancers, who were mostly women, did cartwheels, handstands and back-bends. They danced at banquets and at religious ceremonies, in pairs and in groups. At funerals, *muu*-dancers performed sacred dances which had set steps and movements. These dances were taken very seriously and they had to be learned by heart.

Song
and
Dance

John Malam

W

FRANKLIN WATTS
NEW YORK • LONDON • SYDNEY

© 2000 Franklin Watts

First published in Great Britain by
Franklin Watts
96 Leonard Street
London
EC2A 4XD

Franklin Watts Australia
14 Mars Road
Lane Cove
NSW 2066
Australia

ISBN: 0 7496 3631 9 (hbk)
          0 7496 3772 2 (pbk)
Dewey Decimal Classification 790
A CIP catalogue record for this book is available
from the British Library

Printed in Malaysia
Planning and production by Discovery Books Limited
Editors: Gianna Williams, Samantha Armstrong
Design: Ian Winton
Art Director: Jonathan Hair
Illustrators: Mike White, Joanna Williams,
Stefan Chabluk

Photographs:
4 Bill Leimbach/South American Pictures, 6 R.
Sheridan, 7 top and bottom R. Sheridan/Ancient Art
& Architecture Collection, 8 R. Sheridan/Ancient Art
& Architecture Collection, 9 Michelle Jones/Ancient
Art & Architecture Collection, 10 top & 11 E. T.
Archive, 12 R. Sheridan/Ancient Art & Architecture
Collection, 13 top & bottom E. T. Archive, 14
R.Sheridan/Ancient Art & Architecture Collection,
17 Henrietta Butler/Redferns, 18 top John Taylor
Photographic Ltd, 18 bottom E. T. Archive, 19 top
Pankaj Shah/Redferns, 19 bottom Corbis-Bettman,
21 top & bottom E. T. Archive, 22 top Mary Evans
Picture Library, 22 bottom Corbis-Bettman, 23 E. T.
Archive, 24 Max Jones Files/Redferns, 25 top Mary
Evans Picture Library, 25 bottom Discovery Picture
Library, 26 top Corbis-Bettman, 26 bottom Mick
Hutson/Redferns, 28 Mick Hutson/Redferns,
29 Mary Evans Picture Library.

Acknowledgements
Franklin Watts would like to thank Bang & Olufsen
for the loan of their material.

Contents

Early song and dance

Singing and dancing have been part of everyday life for hundreds of thousands of years. Cave paintings made in Europe 20,000 years ago show us that the people of the Stone Age had dances. They had music too, since their musical instruments have been found.

Dancing and hunting still go together today. Here, the Kayapo people of Brazil dance after a successful hunt.

Dancing in the Stone Age

The people of the Stone Age were hunters. They hunted bison, deer and other wild animals. Hunters dressed in animal skins and danced before they went hunting. Dances were used to bring good luck.

Egyptian music

There were many different musical instruments in Ancient Egypt. Cymbals and bells were shaken, drums and tambourines were beaten, flutes and trumpets were blown and harps and lyres were plucked. People sang songs of worship to the gods, but they also sang songs for fun.

◀▲ Mesopotamian musicians plucked the strings of lyres with their fingertips.

The oldest song

The oldest-known song in the world is almost 3,500 years old. It is a hymn to a Mesopotamian goddess and was sung in the same seven note scale which musicians use today. The song was sung to music played on stringed instruments called lyres.

Music of the gods

By about 1000BC, music was an important part of Ancient Greek culture. The Ancient Greeks believed that song and dance were gifts from the gods. Even musical instruments were said to have been invented by the gods. The Greek philosophers Plato and Aristotle both felt that music should be an important part of a person's education. A musician's skill in playing instruments such as the lyre and *aulos*, a kind of flute, was even judged in musical contests.

This vase shows Greek men enjoying the music of a lyre and an aulos.

A song for every occasion

The Greeks had songs and chants for weddings, births and funerals. Songs were sung at work, and some songs were believed to cure illnesses.

People loved to hear stories about gods and goddesses, and about the adventures of their heroes. Storytellers learned these tales, then recited or sang them to anyone who would listen. Their skill was in telling a favourite story in an exciting way, making up new parts but without changing the meaning. They sang or spoke in a flowing, sing-song rhythm.

Public performances

In Ancient Greece, groups of thirty or more dancers, known as a chorus, danced at festivals. They moved in circles and in lines. As the chorus danced to the music of lyres, they sang songs of praise or victory. Their dances had movements which the audience understood.

Dances with bulls

Bulls were sacred animals to the Minoans, who lived on the Mediterranean island of Crete about 4,000 years ago. This wall painting shows Minoan acrobats holding a bull's horns then somersaulting over its back. Perhaps this was part of a religious dance.

Monks and merry minstrels

Until the AD400s, Greek music had been kept alive in the Roman Empire. But when the Roman Empire disintegrated around AD410, links with the past were broken. During this time of war and chaos, the Christian church kept musical tradition alive and helped develop it.

Chanting in church

Gregorian chant is a style of Christian singing used in monasteries and churches by monks. It is also called plainsong or plainchant, and it was first sung by Christians during the 400s. The monks sang in Latin, which was the language of the Church.

▶ Pope Gregory the Great (540-604) gathered and distributed 3,000 chants throughout the Christian church.

Notation

It was Guido of Arezzo (995-1050) who first invented a system of writing musical notes down. Thanks to this system called notation, melodies that had until then been lost and forgotten could be preserved.

Chant from the past

Cantillation is a chant used by Jewish people in their religious ceremonies. A priest, or rabbi, chants words and phrases which are then repeated by the congregation. Chanting spread from the Holy Land to Europe, where it was copied by the monks of the Middle Ages. It is still used today.

Minstrels

By the 1100s, entertainers called minstrels started to appear in towns across Europe. They were singers and dancers, musicians, jugglers, conjurors and acrobats all rolled into one. They made their living by performing in the streets and at fairs. Some minstrels entertained kings and queens at court.

Minstrels' songs were often funny. Some were rude. Ordinary people liked them, but the Church did not.

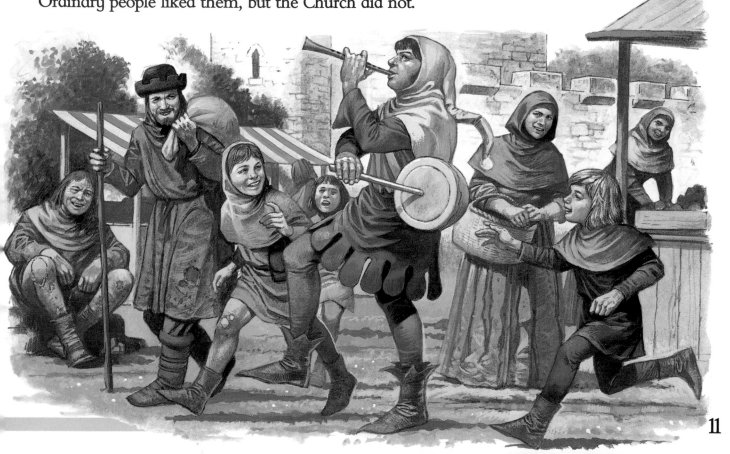

Medieval dance

With the arrival of minstrels, new instruments and written music, dancing became an even more popular part of everyday life.

Folk dancing

Ordinary people at this time enjoyed lively dances with lots of whirling around, clapping and feet stamping. Dancing made them feel happy, and it was an easy way to have fun. Different styles of folk dancing grew up, each with their own movements and music.

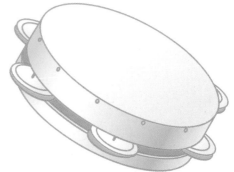

This painting by Brueghel shows peasants dancing in the streets in the late 1500s.

A circle dance of the early 1400s. Dances like this were for members of the nobility.

Court dancing

Members of the nobility had their own, less energetic, dances. They danced in small groups, following set steps they had to learn.

In some French dances of the 1100s, a man and a woman broke away from the group and danced a few steps together. This was quite daring, because until this time men and women had never danced in couples.

Dance of angels

The early Christians had dances at their religious services. Their favourite dance was when people joined hands and danced in a circle. They believed this was how angels danced in heaven. The dancers sang hymns and psalms, clapped their hands and hopped and stamped their feet. This style of dancing in church died out in the twelfth century.

Singing and dancing reached new heights in the 300 years between the 1400s and 1700s, especially at the courts of Europe's kings and queens.

Madrigals

Madrigals were popular from about 1400 to 1600. A madrigal was a poem sung by a group of three to eight singers, who played lutes and recorders. Sometimes one singer sang on his, or her, own.

Madrigals were about love and nature, food and wine. The jester in this painting by Leyster sings on his own.

A royal ball

What dances would you have seen at a ball in King Louis XIV's seventeenth-century France? The first dance was known as a branle. All the men lined up behind the king, and all the women behind the queen. Then, the two long lines of people walked around the room in a set pattern, keeping in step with each other.

The branle dance.

Make a matchbox lute

1 Draw an oblong on the cover of a large empty matchbox. Leave 1 cm all round between the edge and your oblong.

2 Carefully cut the oblong out. Slide the cover back onto the matchbox.

3 Stretch three elastic bands of different widths tightly over the matchbox. Each band will make a different note when plucked.

The next dance was for couples. The king and queen always danced first. Then, when they had finished, it was time for the next couple, and so on until everyone had danced.

Following this was the most popular dance of the time — the minuet. Couples walked on tiptoe around the room, at first dancing near each other, then dancing away in an S or Z pattern. They walked in small steps which made them seem to glide across the floor.

Opera and ballet

Opera and ballet both began in the 1500s, and by the 1700s they were enjoyed by rich and well-educated people in the leading cities of Europe. Composers wrote music for orchestras and singers, and choreographers worked out patterns of steps for dancers.

The audience watches an opera by composer Giuseppe Verdi in the mid-nineteenth century. Some people had private boxes.

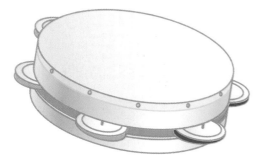

Opera singing

Opera began in Italy. An opera is a play set to music, where the actors and actresses sing their parts instead of speaking them. Operas allowed singers to use the full range of the human voice. They were able to express emotions in ways that singers had not done before.

Grand opera

Grand operas lasted several hours. They had lavish stage effects and a large chorus. The nineteenth-century German composer Richard Wagner (1813-1883) wrote operas to be performed in succession over several days. He built a special opera house of his own in Bayreuth, Germany, to stage them.

Ballet dancing

Ballet began in France. It is a graceful style of dancing. While an orchestra plays music, the dancers tell the story of a play in their movements and steps. One of the most successful ballet composers was the Russian, Piotr Ilyich Tchaikovsky. Many of his ballets, such as *Swan Lake* and *The Nutcracker*, are still among the most performed ballets today.

Tchaikovsky's *The Nutcracker* was first performed in 1892. It is still a popular ballet.

Folk dances

Today, many societies around the world have their own dances. Some are religious dances, some are war dances, while others are folk or country dances. They are passed on from one generation to the next. Many of them originally celebrated important events in the community, such as the harvest or the building of a barn.

An old English folk dance

Once a year, men in the English village of Abbots Bromley, Staffordshire, dance with reindeer antlers. The dance, which is about 800 years old, is a reminder of when the villagers were given the right to hunt in a nearby forest.

The Abbots Bromley horn dance is held on St Bartholomew's Day — the first Sunday after the fourth of September.

A Native American buffalo dance in 1844.

A Native American dance

Native Americans have many dances, each with their own costumes and steps. In the buffalo dance, some of the dancers wear costumes made from buffalo hide while other dancers represent the hunters. The hunters circle round the buffaloes, then pretend to kill them.

Indian classical dance

Indian dances tell stories about love and war. Dancers move their bodies in set ways. Each movement tells a part of the story. Hand and finger movements are very important. In the *Bharat Natya* style of dance, dancers have to know more than fifty different hand and finger positions.

A girl dances the Bharat Natya.

A Maori war dance

Before setting off into battle, the Maoris of New Zealand danced the *haka*. In this dance they shouted, stamped their feet and made warlike gestures with their hands and faces.

Shakers

In the 1700s a religious group began in England called the United Society of Believers in Christ's Second Appearing. Its ideas spread to the United States, and it was there that the group was given the nickname of Shakers. During their meetings, followers danced in circles, swaying and rocking their bodies from side to side.

Songs for the people

Some of the songs we sing today such as the nursery rhymes we hear as children, can be traced back hundreds of years. Other types of everyday song were sung as people worked. But no matter how or when these songs began, they were easy to learn and pass on to others.

Work songs

Sailors sang work songs, called shanties or chanties, while they worked on ships. Singing helped them to concentrate on their work. A shantyman led the singing, and the other sailors joined in with the chorus.
They worked to the rhythm of the song.

Ballads

Rhyming songs that tell stories with lots of verses are called ballads, or laments. Most are sung slowly, and many tell sad stories about hard times and people's misfortunes.

Spirituals

Spirituals were first sung in the USA by African-American slaves. They were sung at work and at religious ceremonies. A leader began the singing, then called out to the people around him to join in at certain places in the song.

Slaves planting sugar cane in the West Indies in 1823.

Nursery rhymes

Often the first songs we hear are nursery rhymes. The best-loved rhymes are hundreds of years old, many of which have surprising origins. 'Humpty Dumpty' dates from the English Civil War (1642–49). Humpty was a cannon which fell to the ground when the wall on which it sat was blown up. 'Ring-a-Ring o' Roses' also dates from the 1600s, when the plague swept through Europe. The first symptom of the plague was the appearance of rose-coloured spots on the skin.

In Victorian times

The late 1800s saw many changes. People looked for new ways to enjoy themselves in their leisure time. This meant trips to the seaside and nights out at the music-hall.

Music-halls

For ordinary people who could not afford to go to the opera or the ballet, the music-hall was a cheap way to enjoy music. Cities and towns built bigger and grander theatres, where audiences were entertained with cheerful songs, juggling acts and comedy sketches. The songs were easy to learn, and audiences were quick to join in.

In 1887, 25 million people watched the shows at London's 300 music-halls.

Capturing sound

In 1877, an American, Thomas Edison (1847–1931), invented a phonograph machine which stored sound on a cylinder covered with tin foil. He called it a phonograph. It was the world's first 'record player'. Manufacturers soon realised how good it would be to record music and then sell it. Until this time all music had to be heard live. In 1889, the first musical recordings went on sale, of piccolo and flute solos.

Music at home

Not everyone went to music-halls. Middle-class families made their own music at home. The family gathered around the piano in the drawing room. Mother played the piano, while the rest of the family sang.

A family sings 'Home Sweet Home', a popular Victorian song.

The waltz

The waltz was an Austrian dance of the 1800s which became popular in ballrooms all over the world. Couples stood face to face with their arms wrapped around one another. At first, it was considered quite daring to hold your partner, but it soon became very popular. It was an easy dance to learn as there were only six steps to know. Couples danced round and round, moving quickly across the dance floor.

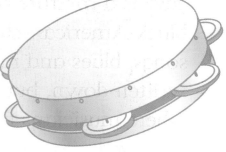

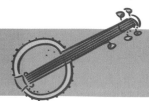

From the start of the 1900s there was a rush of new, popular music, and the birthplace of much of it was America. In the first half of the 1900s many new styles of singing and dancing came into fashion. Some were 'crazes' which soon went out of fashion, but one thing was clear — the twentieth century was a time to have fun.

Rags, blues and jazz

Ragtime tunes, called rags, were for the piano. They were played in 'ragged time' where the tune had an unusual, broken rhythm.

Blues is a kind of black-American folk music, sung in a slow, sad style. A blues song is often sung to music from a guitar, banjo or a mouth organ.

Big bands played swing music, a style of jazz for dancing.

Jazz is a mixture of sounds and rhythms from black-American church music (or gospel), work songs, blues and ragtime. Many jazz tunes are written down, but others rely on improvisation, where musicians make the tunes up as they go along.

Dance crazes

In the 1920s, ballrooms were filled with people dancing the Charleston, cakewalk, turkey trot, chicken scratch and bunny hug. These were energetic dances with lots of wriggling, shaking and twisting movements. Not everyone liked them, and some dances such as the tango were banned because they were too daring for the time!

The tango was first danced in South America in the late 1800s.

Radio – a star is born

Radio was still a new idea at the start of the 1900s. But within a few years, radio stations were broadcasting music programmes. At first, only 'serious' music was broadcast, such as operas, but by the 1920s people were able to enjoy the lively tunes and songs of the day, in the comfort of their own homes. Radio gave music to the people. It kept them up-to-date with all the latest 'hits'.

Music for everyone

In the second half of the twentieth century, radio, cinema and television all broadcast the latest styles of song and dance around the world. Entertainers sang in the open-air to large audiences. Electric instruments changed the style and sound of music, and the use of amplifiers changed the volume!

During the 1950s Elvis Presley (1935-1977) became the 'King' of rock 'n' roll.

Popular music

'Pop' is the name for any kind of popular music. Rock music was first heard in the 1950s, when it was known as rock 'n' roll. Bands have a lead singer and their music is usually played loud. Pop concerts became large events. Some concerts have raised money for good causes.

The crowd dance as a rock band plays in the 1990s.

Protest music

The second half of the twentieth century saw the rise of more serious music as well. There were many different forms of protest music, which expressed young people's anger at modern life. Protest singers in the 1960s played mournful songs while punks in the 1970s thrashed out fast, angry music.

More dance crazes

In the 1950s, young couples danced to rock 'n' roll, spinning their partners through the air. In the 1960s came the twist. In the 1970s disco dancing, with short dance routines, became fashionable. In the 1980s, break-dancers spun on their backs, and in the 1990s people stamped their feet and clapped their hands to Latin-American salsa or cowboy-style line-dancing.

Steel needles to laser beams

For most of the 1900s music was stored on large discs of plastic, called records. To play the music, a steel needle or a small diamond touched the record, which would eventually wear the record out. In the 1980s, compact discs (CDs) began to replace plastic records. A laser beam scans the surface of the CD and 'reads' the music on it. A CD does not wear out as it is only touched by light.

Anything goes!

Today we can watch an opera or a ballet at the theatre, or on television or video at home. We can tune into a song whenever we want to, and if we're not very good at dancing, it doesn't really seem to matter — because nowadays anything goes when you want to have fun.

Karaoke and raves

Anyone can be a three-minute pop-star with help from a karaoke machine. Karaoke is a Japanese word meaning 'empty orchestra'. While the music plays, you read the words on a screen and sing along to your favourite song.

Karaoke singers copy the latest hits.

Today you can dance until dawn at an all-night rave, where there are no rules to follow and no proper steps or movements to learn.

Teenagers pack the dance floor at an all-night rave.

Music and technology

What will singing and dancing be like in the future? We can copy music from the Internet and record it onto CDs in our own homes, and computers can imitate the sounds of musical instruments. Although electronic music will continue to become more sophisticated, people will always feel the need to express their emotions through song and dance.

Modern dance

Modern dance is also called contemporary or experimental dance. It began in the early years of the 1900s, when some dancers, such as Isadora Duncan (1878-1927) began to dance in new ways. She danced barefoot, in loose, free movements. Until this time dancers were taught the steps and movements of classical ballet. It was this style of dancing that modern dance wanted to break away from.

Timeline

BC

c 20,000	People sing and dance to bring good luck in the hunt.
c 6000	In Mesopotamia hymns are sung to gods and goddesses. Music is played on lyres.
c 5000	Egyptians sing and dance at banquets and at religious ceremonies.
c 2000	The Minoans, on the island of Crete, dance with bulls.
c 1500	The oldest-known song in the world is written in Mesopotamia.
c 200	Romans develop their own style of singing and dancing based on Greek and Etruscan styles.

AD

c 400s	Christian monks sing Gregorian chant.
c 800s	Circle dances take place in churches.
c 1000	Music is written down in notation.
c 1100s	Minstrels perform in the streets, and at the courts of kings and queens. In France, the first dances for couples appear.
c 1400s	Madrigals are sung in Europe. Europe's first dancing book was published: *On the Art of Dancing and Directing Choruses*.
c 1500s	The first ballet is danced in France. The first opera is sung in Italy.
c 1600s	Shanties, ballads and work songs are sung by sailors.
c 1700s	The minuet, a dance for couples from France, is the dance of the century.
c 1800s	Music-halls are built in Britain and the USA. The waltz is the most popular dance.
c 1910s	Modern dance, a freer style of dancing than ballet, appears.
c 1920s	People dance the Charleston, the turkey trot and many other routines, to the sounds of jazz music.
c 1940s	Dances from Latin America become fashionable, such as the rumba, samba and cha-cha-cha.
c 1950s	Rock 'n' roll music becomes popular.
c 1960s	The twist is the most popular dance.
c 1970s	Disco dancing becomes popular.
c 1980s	Break-dancing and robotic dancing are popular.
c 1990s	Young people dance at all-night parties, or raves, to house music, a style of electronic music made by computers.

Glossary

Ballad A long, rhyming folk song, sung slowly.

Ballet A form of entertainment in which performers dance and mime to music.

Bull-roarer A simple wind instrument used in the Stone Age.

Cantillation A chant used by Jews in their religious meetings.

Chant Singing, often in church, where verses are spoken in a steady rhythmic way.

Choreographer A person who sets movements to music.

Chorus A group of dancers or singers; also the part of a song repeated between verses.

Composer A person who writes, or composes, music.

Folk Everyday songs or dances, passed on from one generation to the next.

Gospel Black-American music, sung by choirs in churches.

Haka A Maori dance from New Zealand.

Horn dance A folk dance in which animals' horns or antlers are used.

Madrigal Poetry sung by a group of singers.

Minstrel An entertainer of the Middle Ages who could sing and dance.

Music-hall A building in which variety acts were performed in the 1800s and 1900s.

Opera A play set to music.

Plainsong Another name for chant.

Rhythm The timing of a piece of music.

Shanty A work song sung by sailors.

Spiritual A kind of Black-American religious song.

Waltz A ballroom dance of the 1800s.

Further reading

Ardley, Neil, *Eyewitness Guides: Music*, Dorling Kindersley, 1989

Grau, Andree, *Eyewitness Guides: Dance*, Dorling Kindersley, 1998

O'Brien, Eileen, *Story of Music*, Usborne, 1997

Smith, Lucy, *Dance*, Usborne, 1987

Index